Echoes

Aditi Sindwani

BookLeaf Publishing

Presentation by *BookLeaf Publishing*

Web: www.bookleafpub.com

E-mail: info@bookleafpub.com

ISBN: 9789358311235

First edition 2024

DEDICATION

To the Energy that surrounds us all!

ACKNOWLEDGEMENT

I have always been skeptical of my writings, let alone publishing them; however, there have always been a few people in my life who motivated me to continue writing, helping me in editing and giving their valuable suggestions wherever necessary. A special thanks to my family for their endless support; my friends Aarushi, Indirayani, Kriti, Ravindra, Sam, and Shivam for being the best motivators. A special shout out to my sister and Ravindra for pushing me to get them published and Shivam for giving them a read and sharing his valuable inputs.

I would also like to express my gratitude to BookLeaf Publishing for providing such a platform for new poets to get their writings published. Hadn't it been for this opportunity, I would have never taken this step. My publishing consultant Sarah for her endless patience while I took my sweet time to get things done, Lavleen for designing such a beautiful book cover and finally, the editorial team for proofreading it.

Last but not least, my beloved Goddess who gives me the wisdom to convert my thoughts into words.

PREFACE

They say that even silence has its noise! Echoes are the representation of that sound. The sound is non-existent to most, yet it exists for those who care to listen to its rhythm, challenging established norms of society and recounting beautiful stories and wisdom of the sages. Each of its notes traverses through those vast terrains, carried aloft by those relentless and mighty winds.

However, for me, it is not only the voice of utter stillness but also the screams of an appalled heart that is overflooded with streams of emotions and tries to seek peace by reflecting them in words. It is an essence that aims to jolt us into believing and realizing the hope within us and embracing our existence.

Lastly, it is a mirror of sentiments, a song of merry, and a dance of expressions. All this being resonated through every thicket of our existence, projecting what was long lost, forgotten, or ignored.

These verses try to reflect these thoughts that lay dormant for a long time but are in a constant quest to escape into the world and be found out someday by those who are all ears for it.

The Paradox of Fear

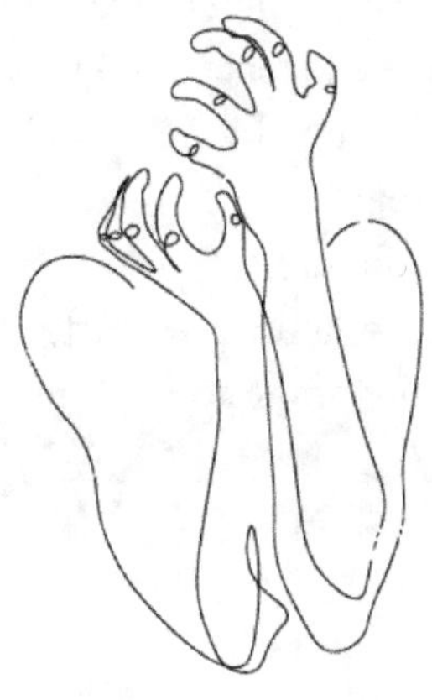

What do you fear the most?
Is it death or misery,
Is it the pain of the broken heart,
Or the ego of the worthless romance?
What is it that ceases us from existing,
Feel the freedom that flows with the wind,
Breathe the life,
That forms the very core of the air,
Surrounding us all the time?
What is it that stops us from walking,
Towards the dream of our life,
Away from the barriers of toxicity,
Bondages of emotions,
And the pain of separation?

What is it that forces us,
To walk the trodden path,
Though full of thorns,
Bleeding our every being of reality,
Making us mere existence of beings,
Living but not being alive?
What is it for real,
Is it the fear of failure,
Or just the pain of a broken heart,
Or the rationality of the folly mind?

Beauty and the Scrounger

What is more beautiful,
The rising of the sun,
Or its setting,
The twinkling of the stars,
Shinning through the thicket blanket,
Of the night sky,
Or the changing shapes of the moon,
Barely reflecting the light,
Enshrined upon it,
On its fellow humans,
Residing on the land,
That it circles day in and day out?
Is it the rustling of the trees,
Dancing to the chords,
Of the wind,
Traversing its path,
Taking away all that is ready,
To be flown away,

By its slight blow?
Or is it the chirping of the birds,
Or the chattering of the animals,
Or an insect's rattling,
Continuously distracting away,
From these thoughts,
That slowly eats up the mind?
What is not beautiful,
About this nature,
Its mountains, valleys, rivers,
The sun, the moon, and the stars,
Its flora, and fauna?
What makes it less beautiful,
Except for the greediness of humans,
Who have always been selflessly endowed,
By her richness,
Slowly and gradually,
Eating it up,
Like a vulture in its might!

The Endless Road

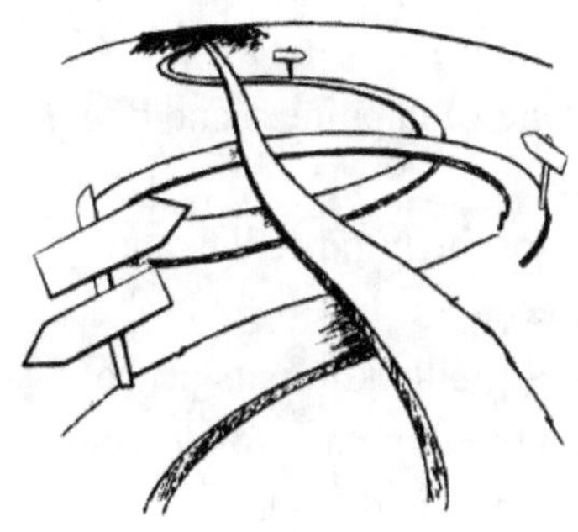

Sometimes the road looks too long,
That it feels tiring,
To even crawl and cross it,
But when the tunnel is darker,
Then what can you do,
Than traveling across it,
In search of light,
That may be found at its end.
A hope of seeing the greens,
On the other end of the road,
Horses galloping,
Being in a race with the winds,
Birds flying freely,
Being a spectator,
Of the competition,

That ensues on the Earth below,
Without any worry,
Of becoming a prisoner,
Of humanity's greed.
A place where the sun shines so bright,
Yet it doesn't itch,
A nomad's land of happiness and hope,
A land where,
All the duels of the mind will evade,
A land where,
The heart will finally know its peace,
A land called the ultimate wonderland,
Of peace, warmth, and hope,
Existing at the end of the tunnel,
That may end someday.

Nowness

Standing on the staircase,
Of a high-rise building,
All isolated from the world,
My mind wanders off,
To the time unknown,
The eras gone by,
The stories that got lost,
With the passing of the wind,
And the laughter that turned,
Into giggles of the closed doors.
It remembers the days that existed before all that
happened,
Before humans were forced to be in cages,
Just like they kept those beloved animals,

For their amusement.
Perhaps it was the dream of a thousand Siamese
cats,
Or the curse of a wrecked soul,
Who knows the true story,
Of the origin of this new beginning.
While being in isolation,
My mind wanders off,
Arousing the craving of my heart,
To pack those stuff again,
And embark on a new journey of self-discovery,
By traveling the path unknown,
Discovering the undiscovered,
And finding a new abode.
It knows now the true essence of life,
The truth of our journeys,
The fact that even if this body is trapped behind
those bars,
It is still free,
Free to travel,
Until its mind knows how to unravel,
The world hidden within its very own depths,
Freeing it from the shackles of its own making,
Understanding the true meaning of freedom,
That until the time our mind is enlightened,
Nothing can truly capture us.

Why Do We Fight?

All this bloodshed,
All this war,
For what interest of ours,
The ones who will not even,
Stay forever to enjoy,
The fruition of their own mind games.
Why cannot we let go of our past,
Our lust for power?
Why cannot we ever choose,
Peace over violence,
Love over hatred?
Why does it always require,
A tower to shatter,
A life to end,

For everything to come in a full circle?
Why cannot we regenerate,
The better version of ourselves,
Rather than trying to make others,
A humanoid of our illusionary world?
No this won't ever work,
Ever stay forever,
As neither evil nor good,
Remains constant,
They are ever-changing,
And will change once again.
Then what are we even fighting for,
When the golden words,
In which we desire our names to be written,
Will too fade away one day.

The Endings

I am just tired right now,
Only if the wind could take me,
To the land of nowhere.
All this hustle and bustle,
All this noise,
All this pain,
Is just bleeding my heart,
Only if it could ever end.
Why does this never end,
Why does this still prevail,
Why does the weather of my heart,
Never change?

If hope is what keeps you alive,
Then why is it slowly dying,
Why distress is what ultimately prevails,
Why does the uneasiness remain?
The questions are numerous,
But none with an answer,
The worries are piling up,
But the resolution is nowhere to be found.
Alas! What would the mind do,
When it doesn't even know,
Which path to take?
All the wisdom and the knowledge,
Feels so small,
That none of them are able to,
Find a resolution,
For this daunting heart.
Everything seems to be nothing,
When it comes to the moment for a tower to fall.

Humanity

What exactly is humanity?
Is it only about being human,
Or being innocent?
Is it about aggression,
Bathed in the ocean of ego,
Or is it about kindness,
Flowing along with the river of sympathy?
Is it all about our fake pride,
That demands unnecessary respect,
Without any return,
And hurting the innocents,
With our arrogance and illusionary knowledge,
Or is it about being gentle,
To the cause of survival,

Having a vision,
That sees everyone as equal,
No more or less than our own existence?

When will this all End?

When will the day arrive,
For the sun to rise again,
Through every street of the living,
Through each and every dark tunnel of
existence,
Leaving behind no living being,
Untouched by its brightness,
Shinning and breathing in this newfound
freedom,
Where a child will laugh,
Without worrying about the future,
Or getting killed and harassed,
For no fault of theirs.
Women will be able to live the life,
The way they want,

Without being told to follow the thinking,
Of the era gone by,
Taking the creators,
Of those rules and regulations,
That defied them of the right to be their own
selves,
Along with itself.
When will we be able to walk again,
Without the fear of being shot,
For having opinions,
Or for having a voice?
When will all of this end,
When will the greed for power end,
When will we be humans for once,
And let other humans be alive for once?

An Anonymous Note

If someone would give me,
That blank note to write,
In anonymity,
I would write all that passed,
The unfulfilled and the unspoken story,
Of my broken heart,
A history that surpassed,
All the pains of the past.
Forming the very core of my existence,
It still exists there,
Pricking and opening the soul,
Forcing it out to venture,
Into the world unknown.
A world to which it never belonged,

But a world that it can never avoid,
As it is that formed the very part,
Of its reality,
And it is what will remain,
Until it arises fully,
From its deep sleep,
To venture out into a new world,
Unbeknownst to its own identity.

The Harsh Reality

Why truth is always so bitter,
And lies so welcoming?
Why does it always break the heart,
When the moment of truth arrives?
Why is it always so difficult,
To accept its existence,
Why is it always so difficult,
To accept the reality?
Why do we always choose,
Darkness over light,
Why do we always choose,
The world of fakeness?
What is so spectacular,
About lies,
That it is so much easier to sing,
Than the worthy lore of honesty and right?

Journey Into Unknown Realms

Where have we arrived,
And where are we led,
Only if the heart ever knew,
To evade the inconveniences of life.
Only if it could ever overcome,
The pain it suffers,
At the hands of its own being.
Walking all blind,
On this road called heaven,
Filled with thorns in the midst of greens,
The cry of heart,
And the screams of mind,
Being mute to those deaf ears,

Slowly burning itself,
In the quest to achieve a château,
The path to which lies deep hidden,
In the forest of existence,
Engulfed by the darkness of malignity.
Only if we ever knew the road to it,
Only if we ever knew the path to follow,
Only if we were ever able to find,
The so-called heaven of realization,
Only if we could ever find that light,
In the midst of noirs.

The Falsify Ego

What are you so proud about,
When you are yet to become invincible?
What is it that you flaunt about,
Those pricey possessions,
That are as tangible as the,
Bubbles in the air,
The knowledge that you have,
When there is still a lot yet to be discovered?
What is it that makes you so aggressive,
That you forget humanity,
The lessons of Empathy and Forgiveness,
And the teachings of Kindness?
What is it that makes you feel so Great,
When you could never see the world,
From other's eyes?
What is it that you are so proud about,
When you are yet to become a butterfly?

What is my Identity?

What defines my character?
What is my identity?
Is it how I talk on the phone,
The clothes I wear,
The way I walk,
Or is it the people I meet,
Or what I celebrate?
Is it only limited,
To the conduct found appropriate,
By the few misguided of the society,
Who in their agony and false pride,
Are ready to destroy,
The very core values of humanity?

Or is it vast and endless,
As the universe in existence,
That has no clear definition,
But doesn't seem to have any limitations as
well?

The Hidden Poison

Why is it so difficult,
To release those emotions,
Of hatred, anger, and jealousy?
Why is it so overbearing,
To forgive and let go,
Of the pains of the past,
Forget those aches,
And laugh away the betrayals,
Of the loved ones?
Why is it so preferable,
To let all these emotions,
Poison your heart,
To the extent,
Where you lose your own self,
To the point of no return,

And becoming deaf for,
Those beautiful soul conversations,
That once defined your life?

The Quest for Acceptance

Why do we need to fit in?
Why do we prefer to lie,
Than just being honest and disliked?
Why showing off is more appreciated,
Than being modest?
Why being true to oneself and others,
Is so difficult than being hidden,
By a mask of falsehood?
Why illusions are so desirable,
Than the bittersweet emotions of life?
Why can't we for once be true to our own
existence,
Standing naked being devoid,
Of any mask of fake emotions,
Breathing happily in the air that flows,

Rejoicing its coolness and calmness,
While talking out loud,
What lies hidden deep within our hearts,
And accepting the reality with an open mind of
ours?

Why is it Always a Fight for Existence?

Why do we need to be more of something,
And less of some other thing?
Why do we need to lose our identity,
To validate our existence?
Why do we need to divide ourselves,
To achieve the very notion of brotherhood?
Why and why do we need,
To make someone inferior,
To feel superior?
Why do we need to pull someone down,
To grow ourselves upward,
Why is it always a fight for existence?
Why is the world always like the Colosseum,
In a constant quest to prove themselves,

Slowly and gradually losing themselves,
In living a life that is a byproduct,
Of their own greed?

A Bird in the Golden Cage

I. Bondage

Trapped in a golden cage,
The eyes look towards,
The world unseen,
Being shrouded by the uncertainty,
Of ever being able to travel,
And fly far-far away,
To her homely abode,
Into the land of Neverland.
These bondages of love,
Are making the heart to shed its sorrows,
Through the passage of eyes,
Continuously raising questions,

About these shackles of life.
Will these chains be ever broken,
Or will the life just end,
Giving way to another bird,
To dance on the same chords,
That once defined her life?

II. The New Found Freedom

The time has arrived,
For the bird to fly,
Leaving behind her golden cage,
In the discovery of Neverland.
But does she still belong to that sky,
She once thought to be her home,
Eyeing every day from the confinement,
Of her golden shell,
In the hope of being a part of what lies beyond,
Becoming one with what is unknown,
Leaving behind the roots of her founding,
To discover the lands of her own?
Or is it just that she has forgotten to fly,
The shackles of her flight,
slowly engulfing her mind,
Turning her present reality,
The belief of her life?

III. Farewell

It is time for her to bid farewell,
To all the mighty highs and their equivalent
lows,
To all the shores and the seas,
To all the worries and the miss.
It is time to go and merge,
Into the land far off,
To go and ditch the forlorn.
It is time for a sweet goodbye,
That the heart doesn't grieve,
But happy to fly away into its land of Neverland.

Being Human

What is it that we feel so guilty about,
why are we afraid to be humans,
Humans that create errors,
That are perfectly imperfect!
Humans, who know nothing,
Yet know everything,
When the time comes.
A human who doesn't shy away,
From fearlessly crying,
Letting the anger, distress, and pain,
Evade like a speck of dust in thin air.
Not afraid to voice their opinions,
And not afraid of others' opinions about them.
What is it that scares us the most,
When we all are alike,

Formed out of the same five elements,
Having the same heart?
What is it that stops us from being our true
selves?
Why can't we accept ourselves for once,
The way we are,
Without the craving to change ourselves,
Per others' liking?
Can't we not stop,
Just for once,
And live our lives in its fullest form?
Can't we just be human for once and all?

The Question of Existence

Why do we always question our identity,
Why do we doubt our existence?
How come we forget,
Our nature of being limitless?
Why do we forget to go beyond?
Why are we so lost,
That we end up questioning our own existence?
When did we end up losing our confidence,
Of being our true selves?
The mind never stops,
Playing games with us,
But how could we just let it do so,
And if we can't even make that to stop,
Are we even that great,
To be called an existence immensely evolved?

The invincible intelligent beings,
Ruling this planet,
And being the kings,
Of everyone's lives?
Only if we could ever learn,
To be human?
Only if we could learn,
To not rule but serve,
And only if we could learn,
To live once again,
Being completely drowned,
In the heavenly sentiments of,
Empathy and sympathy,
Only and only if we could know,
What is it to be true to our own existence?

Ignorance

And one day I just quit,
Leaving all that was there,
The pain and the joy of life,
Into the misty planes of time.
But no one ever asked me the reason,
No one ever bothered,
To know the stimulation.
They rather chose to be the teacher,
Of the Karma of Life,
Continuously blabbering the mantra of 'All that
Suffice'.
Is life really that simple,
A question that the soul never ceased to ask,
And a question that no one could ever answer,

Yet insisted on the beauty of life.
The mind got confused,
Being bombarded by the wisdom,
Of all those self-proclaimed sages of society,
Trying to make meaning out of what was being
said,
And what was being felt.
It wanted to ask everyone out there,
The solution to this mystery of life,
About the dreadfulness of this existence,
If all that existed was truly so alluring.
Alas! That it could never find the answer,
To this endless questions of life,
As the yores that preached of it,
Were lost in a quest to resolve,
The mysteries of time.
The mind at last grievingly settled down,
Silently downloading what was being said,
Deep into its marshes of melancholy,
So as to teach its kid,
The beauty of life that exists.

Why are We so Lost?

Why are we so much into the future,
That we forget to think about the present?
Why are we always running around,
That we forget to smile,
While rejoicing in those small moments,
For which we worked so hard?
Why are we always stressing around,
Forgetting the happiness we got,
From the laughter that came,
After the crying of a kid who fell down?
Why privacy has become such a mandate,
That we forget to embrace the beauty of,
Spending time with fellow actors?
Why have we become so busy,
That even the chance to,
Calmly watch those beloved mountains,
Has become a pricey commodity?